. tiny book of .

PIES

Pecan Pie

1 cup white corn syrup
1/3 cup light brown sugar
1/3 teaspoon salt
1/3 cup melted butter
1 teaspoon vanilla
3 whole eggs
1 cup pecans
1 nine in...
Pre-...

Coconut Pie

1 pt Half + Half
1 cup sugar
1 pinch salt
1 teaspoon vanilla
3 egg yolks
1½ tbs corn starch
½ stick butter
...

Strawberry Pie

... sugar
... tablespoon corn starch
...up water
...teaspoon lemon rine
...up mashed strawberries
...ix the above together and
... 1 minutes or until
... and color. Le...

.tiny book of.
PIES

Classic Recipes *for* Every Season

Small Pleasures™
· SERIES ·

hm | books

Small Pleasures™
· SERIES ·
hm|books

AUTHOR *Cindy Smith Cooper*
ART DIRECTOR *Cailyn Haynes*

EDITORIAL
CREATIVE DIRECTOR/PHOTOGRAPHY *Mac Jamieson*
RECIPE EDITOR *Fran Jensen*
COPY EDITORS *Avery Hurt, Emma Pitts*
STYLIST *Lucy Herndon*
SENIOR PHOTOGRAPHERS *John O'Hagan,*
Marcy Black Simpson
PHOTOGRAPHERS *Jim Bathie, William Dickey,*
Stephanie Welbourne
ASSISTANT PHOTOGRAPHER *Caroline Smith*
FOOD STYLISTS/RECIPE DEVELOPERS *Mary-Claire Britton,*
Melissa Gray, Kathleen Kanen, Janet Lambert,
Vanessa Rocchio, Emily Turner, Loren Wood
TEST KITCHEN ASSISTANT *Anita Simpson Spain*
SENIOR DIGITAL IMAGING SPECIALIST *Delisa McDaniel*
DIGITAL IMAGING SPECIALIST *Clark Densmore*

hm
hoffmanmedia

CHAIRMAN OF THE BOARD/CEO *Phyllis Hoffman DePiano*
PRESIDENT/COO *Eric W. Hoffman*
PRESIDENT/CCO *Brian Hart Hoffman*
EXECUTIVE VICE PRESIDENT/CFO *Mary P. Cummings*
EXECUTIVE VICE PRESIDENT/O&M *Greg Baugh*
VICE PRESIDENT/DIGITAL MEDIA *Jon Adamson*
VICE PRESIDENT/EDITORIAL *Cindy Smith Cooper*
VICE PRESIDENT/IMS *Ray Reed*
VICE PRESIDENT/ADMINISTRATION *Lynn Lee Terry*

Hoffman Media
1900 International Park Drive, Suite 50
Birmingham, Alabama 35243
www.hoffmanmedia.com
ISBN # 978-1-940772-35-6
Printed in China

ON THE COVER:
(Front) Coconut Lemon Pie, page 14.
(Back) Mini Peach Cobblers, page 125.

.contents.

.introduction.

Who can say no to dessert as a sweet ending to a meal, or just a treat with coffee?

PIE IS ONE OF THE MOST COMFORTING FOODS—everyone loves to eat pie! As one of the easier desserts to prepare, there are as many pie variations as there are ingredients. Every fruit—and even some vegetables like the pumpkin—has been sweetened into pie form and given an interesting name or personalized to suit its baker. Chocolate, nuts, and even peppermint have made their way into pies! Whether you serve your pie warm or chilled, you'll find a variety of options throughout the pages of this delightful book.

The pastry is just as good as the filling and can be my favorite part—with no crumbs left on the plate! Single- or double-crust, the pastry holds the goodness of the pie within. I have heard cooks say that decorating the pie top is their favorite part of making pies. Cutouts for holidays and seasons, like leaf shapes for fall, can be used to encircle the pie edges. Or like Mother, you might just like to make an impression with fork tines. It also helps to seal the pastry to the pie plate before baking.

From classics like Coconut Cream Pie to a scrumptious White Chocolate and Toasted Nut Tart, you will be able to include any of your favorite ingredients in a delicious pie. Easy to transport for parties and celebrations, even the hand pies will have a place in your heart for years to come. Enjoy some of our best pies, and be ready for the compliments and requests for more.

— *Cindy*

Basic Pie Dough

MAKES 2 (9-INCH) PIECRUSTS

In the work bowl of a food processor, pulse together flour, sugar, and salt. Add butter, and pulse until mixture is crumbly, about 1 minute. With processor running, add 3/4 cup ice water in a slow, steady stream until mixture forms a dough.

Turn out dough, and shape into 2 disks. Wrap each disk in plastic wrap, and refrigerate until firm, about 2 hours.

4 cups all-purpose flour
1/2 cup sugar
1/2 teaspoon kosher salt
12 tablespoons cold unsalted butter, cubed
3/4 cup ice water

Buttermilk Pie Dough

MAKES 1 (9-INCH) PIECRUST

In a medium bowl, whisk together flour, sugar, and salt. Using a pastry blender, cut in butter until mixture is crumbly. Add buttermilk, 1 tablespoon at a time, stirring until a dough forms.

Turn out dough, and shape into a disk. Wrap in plastic wrap, and refrigerate for at least 1 hour.

- 1¼ cups all-purpose flour
- 1 teaspoon sugar
- 1 teaspoon kosher salt
- ½ cup unsalted butter, cubed
- 3 to 4 tablespoons whole buttermilk, chilled

Classic
PIES

TRADITIONAL OLD FAVORITES WITH
NEW TWISTS, CROWNED WITH A VARIETY
OF FLAVORS FROM TOASTED COCONUT
MERINGUE TO GRANOLA CRUMBLES

Coconut Lemon Pie

CRUST
1⅓ cups all-purpose flour
1 tablespoon sugar
½ teaspoon salt
3 tablespoons cold
    unsalted butter,
    cubed
3 tablespoons all-
    vegetable shortening
4 to 5 tablespoons
    ice water

FILLING
½ cup sugar
½ cup all-purpose flour
2¼ cups whole milk
4 large egg yolks
1 cup sweetened
    flaked coconut
3 tablespoons butter
2 teaspoons lemon zest
2 tablespoons fresh
    lemon juice
Meringue (recipe follows)
Garnish: toasted
    sweetened flaked
    coconut

MERINGUE
MAKES ABOUT 4 CUPS

1 cup sugar
4 large egg whites,
    room temperature

CRUST In a large bowl, whisk together flour, sugar, and salt. Cut in butter and shortening until mixture is crumbly. Add ice water, 1 tablespoon at a time, just until moistened. Turn out dough, and shape into a disk. Wrap in plastic wrap, and refrigerate for at least 1 hour. Preheat oven to 400°. On a lightly floured surface, roll dough to a 12-inch circle. Transfer to a 9-inch pie plate, pressing into bottom and up sides. Fold edges under, and crimp as desired. Prick bottom and sides of dough with a fork. Top with a piece of parchment paper. Add pie weights. Bake until edges of crust begin to brown, about 20 minutes. Reduce oven temperature to 375°. Carefully remove paper and weights. Bake until lightly browned, about 20 minutes more. Let cool completely.

FILLING In a large saucepan, stir together sugar and flour; whisk in milk. Cook over medium heat until thick and bubbly, stirring constantly. Remove from heat. In a medium bowl, place egg yolks; whisk in 1 cup hot milk mixture. Return egg yolk mixture to remaining hot milk mixture. Cook until thick and bubbly, stirring constantly. Remove from heat. Add coconut, butter, lemon zest, and lemon juice; stir until butter is melted. Spoon mixture into prepared crust. Place a piece of plastic wrap directly on surface of filling. Refrigerate until chilled, about 3 hours. Spoon Meringue onto center of filling, spreading to within 1 inch of crust. Using your fingers, pull Meringue into tall peaks. Using a kitchen torch, lightly brown top of Meringue. Garnish with coconut, if desired.

MERINGUE In the top of a double boiler, whisk together sugar and egg whites. Cook over simmering water, whisking constantly, until sugar is dissolved and egg whites are warm to the touch, 3 to 4 minutes. Transfer to the bowl of a stand mixer fitted with the whisk attachment. Beat at low speed for 2 minutes. Increase mixer speed to high, and beat until stiff peaks form and mixture cools, about 6 minutes.

Recipe TIP

You may also place meringue-topped pie 2 inches from a hot broiler until meringue is lightly browned. If you use this method, be sure to use a pie plate that is broilerproof.

Classic Pecan Pie

Preheat oven to 350°.

On a lightly floured surface, roll Buttermilk Pie Dough to ⅛-inch thickness. Transfer to a 9-inch pie plate, pressing into bottom and up sides. Fold edges under, and crimp as desired.

In a medium bowl, stir together eggs, brown sugar, corn syrup, melted butter, vanilla, and salt. Gently stir in pecans. Pour mixture into prepared crust.

Bake for 30 minutes. Loosely cover with foil, and bake until center is set, about 20 minutes more. Let cool completely on a wire rack.

MAKES 1 (9-INCH) PIE

**Buttermilk Pie Dough
(recipe on page 11)**
3 large eggs
**1 cup firmly packed light
brown sugar**
¾ cup light corn syrup
**½ cup unsalted butter,
melted and cooled**
1 teaspoon vanilla extract
1 teaspoon kosher salt
2 cups pecan halves

'Pecan' is pronounced two different ways, causing a jovial conversation about who is correct. Pee-can or puh-kahn! The trees can live up to 300 years, making wonderful shade trees and a reliable source of delicious pecans for generations. Toasted, pecans are a healthy snack and suitable to serve at any occasion.

Caramel Apple Pie

**1 (14.1-ounce)
package refrigerated
piecrusts**
**6 cups peeled, cored,
and thinly sliced
Granny Smith or
Gala apples (about
6 medium apples)**
**⅓ cup prepared
caramel sauce, plus
more for serving**
¼ cup sugar
**3 tablespoons all-
purpose flour**
**½ teaspoon ground
cinnamon**
¼ teaspoon salt
**1 tablespoon unsalted
butter, cubed**
1 teaspoon water

Preheat oven to 400°.

On a lightly floured surface, roll half of dough to a 12-inch circle. Transfer to a 9-inch pie plate, pressing into bottom and up sides.

In a large bowl, toss together apples, caramel sauce, sugar, flour, cinnamon, and salt. Spoon apple mixture into prepared crust; top with butter. Brush edges of crust with 1 teaspoon water.

On a lightly floured surface, roll remaining dough to a 12-inch circle. Place dough over apple mixture. Trim edges, fold edges of both crusts under, and crimp as desired. Cut several 1-inch vents in top of dough to release steam.

Bake until crust is golden brown and filling is bubbly, 40 to 45 minutes, covering with foil during last 15 minutes of baking to prevent excess browning, if necessary. Let cool completely on a wire rack. Serve with additional caramel sauce.

The saying "As American as apple pie" and the childhood story about Johnny Appleseed have supported the popularity of this dessert.

Buttermilk Chess Pie

Preheat oven to 350°.

On a lightly floured surface, roll Basic Pie Dough to a 12-inch circle. Transfer to a 9-inch pie plate, pressing into bottom and up sides. Fold edges under, and crimp as desired.

In a medium bowl, whisk together sugar, flour, cornmeal, and salt. In another medium bowl, whisk eggs. Add sugar mixture to eggs, whisking to combine.

In a small bowl, combine buttermilk, yogurt, and lemon juice, whisking until smooth. Add melted butter and vanilla. Gradually add buttermilk mixture to sugar mixture, whisking after each addition. Pour mixture into prepared crust.

Bake for 20 minutes; loosely cover with foil, and bake until filling is set and top of pie is light golden brown, 20 to 25 minutes more. Let cool completely on a wire rack. Cover and refrigerate for up to 5 days.

MAKES 1 (9-INCH) PIE

- ½ recipe Basic Pie Dough (recipe on page 10)
- 1 cup sugar
- 3 tablespoons all-purpose flour
- 1½ tablespoons yellow cornmeal
- ½ teaspoon salt
- 5 large eggs, room temperature
- ¾ cup whole buttermilk, room temperature
- 3 tablespoons plain Greek yogurt
- 1 tablespoon fresh lemon juice
- ⅓ cup butter, melted and cooled
- 2 teaspoons vanilla extract

The chess pie is a classic of Southern cuisine, available at many restaurants and cafes alike for dessert. Its use of cornmeal sets it apart from the traditional custard-type pie.

Pumpkin Pie with Granola Crumble

MAKES 1 (9-INCH) PIE

1 (14.1-ounce) package
   refrigerated piecrusts
2 (15-ounce) cans pumpkin
3 large eggs, lightly beaten
½ cup granulated sugar
½ cup firmly packed light
   brown sugar
½ cup heavy whipping cream
1 teaspoon pumpkin pie spice
1 teaspoon vanilla extract
½ teaspoon ground ginger
¼ teaspoon salt
¼ teaspoon ground cardamom
Granola Crumble (recipe
   follows)
Garnish: sweetened dried
   cranberries*

*We used Craisins.

GRANOLA CRUMBLE
MAKES ABOUT 1¼ CUPS

½ cup all-purpose flour
½ cup prepared granola
¼ cup sliced almonds
¼ cup firmly packed light
   brown sugar
½ teaspoon ground cinnamon
¼ teaspoon salt
6 tablespoons unsalted butter,
   melted

Preheat oven to 350°. Line a baking sheet with parchment paper.

On a lightly floured surface, roll half of dough to a 12-inch circle. Transfer to a 9-inch pie plate, pressing into bottom and up sides.

Roll remaining dough to ¼-inch thickness. Using a 1½-inch maple leaf cutter, cut dough, rerolling scraps as necessary. Place on prepared pan. Bake until golden brown, 10 to 15 minutes. Let cool completely.

In a medium bowl, whisk together pumpkin, eggs, granulated sugar, brown sugar, cream, pumpkin pie spice, vanilla, ginger, salt, and cardamom. Pour mixture into prepared crust.

Bake until filling is set, 35 to 40 minutes. Remove from oven; add Granola Crumble to top of pie. Bake until crumble is golden brown, about 15 minutes more. Let cool completely on a wire rack. Garnish with prepared maple leaves and cranberries, if desired.

GRANOLA CRUMBLE In a small bowl, combine flour, granola, almonds, brown sugar, cinnamon, and salt. Add melted butter, stirring just until combined. Store in an airtight container in refrigerator for up to 1 week.

Coconut Cream Pie

Preheat oven to 425°. Spray a 9-inch pie plate with baking spray with flour.

On a lightly floured surface, roll dough to a 12-inch circle. Transfer to prepared pie plate, pressing into bottom and up sides. Fold edges under, and crimp as desired. Prick bottom and sides of dough with a fork. Top with a piece of parchment paper, letting ends extend over edges of plate. Add pie weights.

Bake until lightly browned, 12 to 15 minutes. Carefully remove paper and weights. Let cool completely.

In a medium saucepan, whisk together sugar and cornstarch. Add half-and-half and eggs, whisking until smooth. Cook over medium heat, whisking constantly, until mixture comes to a boil and thickens, about 15 minutes. Remove from heat; stir in 1 cup toasted coconut and vanilla.

Pour mixture into prepared crust. Cover and refrigerate for at least 2 hours or up to 3 days. Just before serving, spread whipped topping over pie, sealing to edges.

Sprinkle with remaining ½ cup toasted coconut.

MAKES 1 (9-INCH) PIE

½ (14.1-ounce) package
    refrigerated
    piecrusts
¾ cup sugar
¼ cup cornstarch
3 cups half-and-half
3 large eggs
1½ cups sweetened
    flaked coconut,
    toasted and divided
1 teaspoon vanilla
    extract
1 (8-ounce) container
    frozen whipped
    topping, thawed

Black Bottom Banana Cream Pie

½ cup plus 2 tablespoons
   butter, divided
2 cups chocolate graham
   cracker crumbs
1 cup sugar, divided
1¼ (4-ounce) bars
   semisweet baking
   chocolate, chopped
⅓ cup heavy whipping
   cream
3 to 4 ripe bananas,
   sliced ¼ inch thick
1½ cups half-and-half
1 teaspoon vanilla extract
2 tablespoons cornstarch
2 large eggs
1 large egg yolk
1 (8-ounce) container
   frozen whipped
   topping, thawed

In a small microwave-safe bowl, melt ½ cup butter. In a medium bowl, combine graham cracker crumbs, ½ cup sugar, and melted butter. Using a measuring cup, press mixture into bottom and up sides of a 9-inch pie plate. Refrigerate for at least 15 minutes.

In a medium bowl, place chopped chocolate. In a small saucepan, bring cream and remaining 2 tablespoons butter to a boil over medium-high heat. Remove from heat, and pour over chopped chocolate. Whisk until smooth. Pour into prepared crust, and refrigerate for at least 30 minutes. Arrange banana slices over chocolate layer.

In a medium saucepan, combine half-and-half and vanilla. Cook over medium heat, stirring frequently, until mixture begins to simmer, 3 to 5 minutes.

In a medium bowl, whisk together cornstarch and remaining ½ cup sugar. Add eggs and egg yolk, whisking until smooth. Gradually add hot half-and-half mixture to egg mixture, whisking well after each addition. Transfer mixture to saucepan, and continue to cook over medium heat, stirring constantly, until mixture comes to a boil and thickens, about 6 minutes. Boil for 1 minute. Strain through a fine-mesh sieve into another medium bowl. Refrigerate for 20 minutes. Spread mixture over banana layer. Refrigerate pie for 2 to 4 hours.

Top with whipped topping. Refrigerate for up to 3 days.

Butterscotch Pie

Preheat oven to 350°.

On a lightly floured surface, roll dough to a 12-inch circle. Transfer to a 9-inch pie plate, pressing into bottom and up sides. Fold edges under, and crimp as desired. Top with a piece of parchment paper, letting ends extend over edges of plate. Add pie weights.

Bake for 15 minutes. Carefully remove paper and weights. Bake until golden brown, about 5 minutes more.

In a medium saucepan, whisk together sugar, cornstarch, and salt. In a small bowl, whisk together egg yolks and milk. Whisk egg mixture into sugar mixture. Bring to a boil over medium heat, stirring constantly. Cook for 1 minute, stirring constantly. Remove from heat. Add butter, butterscotch, and vanilla, stirring until smooth.

Pour mixture into prepared crust. Place a piece of plastic wrap directly on surface of filling. Refrigerate until chilled, about 4 hours. Garnish with whipped topping, if desired.

Makes 1 (9-inch) pie

- ½ (14.1-ounce) package refrigerated piecrusts
- ½ cup sugar
- 3 tablespoons cornstarch
- ⅛ teaspoon kosher salt
- 4 large egg yolks
- 2 cups whole milk
- ¼ cup unsalted butter, cubed
- 1 (12-ounce) package butterscotch morsels
- 1 teaspoon vanilla extract
- Garnish: frozen whipped topping, thawed

The main ingredients for butterscotch are butter and brown sugar. It reminds me of butterscotch candy in the familiar yellow wrapper in the candy dish.

Cherry Pie

MAKES 1 (9-INCH) PIE

CRUST
4 cups all-purpose flour
½ cup sugar
½ cup ground toasted almonds
½ teaspoon salt
10 tablespoons cold unsalted butter, cubed
⅔ cup ice water

FILLING
2 pounds pitted fresh cherries
½ cup plus 2 tablespoons sugar, divided
¼ cup cornstarch
3 tablespoons water
1 teaspoon vanilla extract
½ teaspoon kosher salt
1 large egg, lightly beaten

CRUST In the work bowl of a food processor, pulse together flour, sugar, almonds, and salt. Add butter, pulsing until mixture is crumbly, about 20 seconds. With processor running, add ⅔ cup ice water in a slow, steady stream until mixture forms a dough. Turn out dough, and shape into 2 disks. Wrap each disk in plastic wrap, and refrigerate for at least 1 hour.

FILLING In a large saucepan, combine cherries and ½ cup sugar over medium-high heat. Cook, stirring occasionally, until sugar dissolves.

In a small bowl, whisk together cornstarch and 3 tablespoons water. Add cornstarch mixture to cherries, stirring constantly. Add vanilla and salt. Reduce heat to medium, and continue cooking until mixture thickens and coats the back of a wooden spoon. Remove from heat.

Preheat oven to 350°. On a lightly floured surface, roll half of dough to a 12-inch circle. Transfer to a 9-inch pie plate, pressing into bottom and up sides. Trim excess dough to ½-inch beyond edge of plate. Fold edges under, and crimp as desired. Prick bottom and sides of dough with a fork. Bake until edges are barely golden, about 15 minutes. Spoon cherry mixture into prepared crust.

Roll remaining dough to ⅛-inch thickness. Using a pastry wheel or a knife, cut 1-inch-wide strips. Arrange in a lattice design over cherry mixture. Trim strips even with edges, and press together. Brush dough with egg, and sprinkle with remaining 2 tablespoons sugar. Bake until crust is golden brown, 20 to 25 minutes. Let cool before serving.

Peanut Butter Pie

1 (5-ounce) sleeve cinnamon
    graham crackers (about
    9 whole crackers)
1 cup salted roasted peanuts
2 tablespoons sugar
6 tablespoons butter,
    slightly softened
1½ cups creamy peanut butter
1 (8-ounce) package cream
    cheese, softened
1 cup confectioners' sugar,
    sifted
2 cups heavy whipping cream
Garnish: chopped peanuts,
    sweetened whipped
    cream

Recipe TIP

Make it mile high! We love
our Peanut Butter Pie served
with a bounty of sweetened
whipped cream on top. You
can even drizzle prepared
chocolate sauce on it, too!

Preheat oven to 350°. Lightly spray a 9-inch pie plate with cooking spray.

In the work bowl of a food processor, combine graham crackers, peanuts, and sugar; pulse until finely ground, 5 to 6 times. Add butter; pulse until blended, 3 to 4 times. Reserve 1 tablespoon crumb mixture for garnish. Using a measuring cup, press remaining mixture into bottom and up sides of prepared pie plate.

Bake until lightly browned, about 10 minutes. Let cool completely.

In a large bowl, beat peanut butter and cream cheese with a mixer at medium speed until smooth, stopping to scrape sides of bowl. Add confectioners' sugar, beating to combine. Add cream; beat at low speed until combined. Increase mixer speed to high; beat just until mixture is thickened. (Do not overbeat.)

Spread filling into prepared crust. Cover and refrigerate until firm, about 4 hours. Garnish with reserved 1 tablespoon crumb mixture, peanuts, and whipped cream, if desired.

Lattice-Topped Blueberry Pie

Make Basic Pie Dough, adding thyme and cinnamon to dry ingredients, if desired. Preheat oven to 350°. On a lightly floured surface, roll half of dough to a 12-inch circle, about ⅛-inch thick. Transfer to a 9-inch deep-dish pie plate, pressing into bottom and up sides. Trim edges to ¼-inch beyond edge of plate. Cover and refrigerate for 30 minutes.

Roll remaining dough to an 11-inch circle, about ⅛-inch thick. Cut into 12 (¾-inch-wide) strips. Transfer to a baking sheet, cover with plastic wrap and refrigerate for 15 minutes. Prick bottom and sides of pie dough with a fork. Bake until edges are pale, 12 to 16 minutes. In a large stockpot, heat blueberries and ½ cup sugar over medium heat. Cook, stirring occasionally, until most berries pop, 8 to 12 minutes. Strain berries through a fine-mesh sieve set over a bowl, reserving berries and juice.

In a medium bowl, whisk together 1 cup reserved blueberry juice, ½ cup sugar, tapioca flour, and salt. Add strained blueberries to juice mixture, stirring gently to combine. Pour blueberry mixture into prepared crust.

Place 6 dough strips vertically over pie, using longer strips in center and shorter ones on sides. Fold back every other strip to its midway point. Place a new strip crosswise over unfolded strips. Unfold vertical strips, crossing horizontal one. Fold back alternating strips, and place another crosswise strip parallel to first one. Continue weaving in this fashion until you have 3 crosswise strips on this half of pie. Weave crust on remaining half of pie in the same fashion.

Brush dough strips with cream, and sprinkle with remaining 2 tablespoons sugar. Place pie on a rimmed baking sheet. Bake until filling is bubbly and crust is golden, about 1 hour. Let cool for at least 3 hours before serving.

MAKES 1 (9-INCH)
DEEP-DISH PIE

**Basic Pie Dough
(recipe on page 10)**
**1 tablespoon minced
fresh thyme
(optional)**
**1½ teaspoons ground
cinnamon (optional)**
6 pints fresh blueberries
**1 cup plus 2 tablespoons
sugar, divided**
¼ cup tapioca flour
½ teaspoon kosher salt
**2 tablespoons heavy
whipping cream**

Chocolate Cream Pie

Makes 1 (9-inch) pie

CRUST
½ **(14.1-ounce) package**
  refrigerated piecrusts

FILLING
½ **cup sugar**
3 tablespoons cornstarch
⅛ **teaspoon kosher salt**
2½ **cups whole milk**
5 large egg yolks
4 tablespoons unsalted
  butter, cubed
1 (4-ounce) bar
  semisweet chocolate,
  chopped
½ **(4-ounce) bar**
  unsweetened baking
  chocolate, chopped
2 teaspoons vanilla
  extract

TOPPING
2 cups heavy whipping
  cream
⅓ **cup sugar**
1 tablespoon prepared
  hot fudge sauce

Preheat oven to 350°.

CRUST On a lightly floured surface, roll dough to a 12-inch circle. Transfer to a 9-inch pie plate, pressing into bottom and up sides. Fold edges under, and crimp as desired. Top with a piece of parchment paper, letting ends extend over edges of plate. Add pie weights.

Bake until golden brown, about 25 minutes. Carefully remove paper and weights. Let cool for 10 minutes.

FILLING In a medium saucepan, whisk together sugar, cornstarch, and salt. Add milk and egg yolks, whisking to combine. Bring to a boil over medium heat, stirring constantly. Cook, stirring constantly, until thickened and bubbly, about 2 minutes. Reduce heat to low. Stir in butter, 1 tablespoon at a time, until combined. Gradually add chocolate, stirring until melted. Remove from heat. Stir in vanilla.

Spoon filling into prepared crust. Let cool for 10 minutes. Place a piece of plastic wrap directly on surface of filling. Refrigerate until firm, about 3 hours.

TOPPING In a medium bowl, beat cream and sugar with a mixer at high speed until stiff peaks form. Top pie with whipped cream. Drop teaspoonfuls of hot fudge sauce over whipped cream. Using the back of a spoon, swirl into whipped cream.

Fruit
PIES

SWEETENED AND SPICED FRESH FRUITS
PROVIDE COLORFUL FILLINGS FOR THESE
RECTANGULAR, ROUND, AND SLAB PIES

Blackberry-Blueberry Pie

MAKES 1 (9-INCH) PIE

**2 recipes Buttermilk Pie
Dough (recipe on
page 11)**
3 cups fresh blackberries
3 cups fresh blueberries
**¾ cup plus 2 teaspoons
sugar, divided**
6 tablespoons cornstarch
**1 tablespoon fresh
lemon juice**
¼ teaspoon kosher salt
**2 tablespoons cold
unsalted butter,
cubed**
**1 tablespoon half-and-
half**

Preheat oven to 400°.

On a lightly floured surface, roll half of Buttermilk Pie Dough
to a 12-inch circle. Transfer to a 9-inch pie plate, pressing
into bottom and up sides, letting excess dough extend over
edges of plate. Brush edges of dough with water.

In a large bowl, gently stir together blackberries,
blueberries, ¾ cup sugar, cornstarch, lemon juice, and
salt. Spoon into prepared crust; sprinkle with butter.

On a lightly floured surface, roll remaining dough to a
12-inch circle. Using a paring knife, cut 6 to 8 leaf shapes
in center of dough, spacing 1-inch apart; discard scraps.
Place dough over berry mixture, pressing edges together.
Trim excess dough; fold edges under, and crimp as desired.
Brush with half-and-half, and sprinkle with remaining
2 teaspoons sugar.

Bake for 15 minutes. Reduce oven temperature to 350°,
and bake until golden brown, about 45 minutes more,
loosely covering with foil to prevent excess browning,
if necessary. Let cool completely on a wire rack.

*Blueberries can be sprinkled into cereal for breakfast,
layered with yogurt as a dessert, or dropped
into a morning smoothie—frozen or plain.*

Blueberry-Plum Slab Pie

Preheat oven to 400°. Line a 15x10-inch rimmed baking sheet with parchment paper.

On a lightly floured surface, roll half of Slab Pie Dough into an 18x13-inch rectangle. Transfer to prepared pan, pressing into corners and letting excess dough extend over edges. Freeze for 10 minutes.

In a large bowl, stir together blueberries, plums, granulated sugar, tapioca flour, zest, and salt. Spread mixture onto prepared crust, leaving a 1-inch border.

On a lightly floured surface, roll remaining dough into a 16x11-inch rectangle. Place over filling. Fold edges under, and crimp as desired. Cut several 1-inch slits in top of dough to release steam. Brush with egg, and sprinkle with turbinado sugar.

Bake for 15 minutes. Reduce oven temperature to 350°, and bake until crust is golden brown and filling is bubbly, about 45 minutes more, loosely covering with foil to prevent excess browning, if necessary. Let cool completely on a wire rack.

SLAB PIE DOUGH In the work bowl of a food processor, pulse together flour, sugar, and salt. Add butter, pulsing until mixture is crumbly, about 30 seconds. With processor running, add 3/4 cup cold water in a slow, steady stream until a dough forms.

Turn out dough, and shape into 2 disks. Wrap tightly in plastic wrap, and refrigerate for at least 1 hour.

MAKES 1 (15x10-INCH) PIE

Slab Pie Dough (recipe follows)
5 cups fresh blueberries
5 cups pitted sliced fresh plums
3/4 cup granulated sugar
1/4 cup tapioca flour
1/2 teaspoon orange zest
1/2 teaspoon kosher salt
1 large egg, lightly beaten
1 tablespoon turbinado sugar

SLAB PIE DOUGH
MAKES 2 PIECRUSTS

4 cups all-purpose flour
1/2 cup sugar
2 teaspoons kosher salt
12 tablespoons cold unsalted butter, cubed
3/4 cup cold water

Strawberry Pie

**Buttermilk Pie Dough
    (recipe on page 11)**
1 cup sugar
2 tablespoons cornstarch,
    sifted
1 cup boiling water
1 teaspoon strawberry extract
½ teaspoon vanilla extract
1 (3-ounce) box strawberry
    gelatin
2 quarts fresh strawberries,
    halved

Preheat oven to 350°.

On a lightly floured surface, roll Buttermilk Pie Dough to a 12-inch circle. Transfer to a 9-inch pie plate, pressing into bottom and up sides. Fold edges under, and crimp as desired. Top with a piece of parchment paper, letting ends extend over edges of plate. Add pie weights.

Bake for 15 minutes. Carefully remove paper and weights. Bake until golden brown, about 15 minutes more. Let cool for 10 minutes.

In a small saucepan, whisk together sugar and cornstarch. Add 1 cup boiling water, strawberry extract, and vanilla. Cook over medium heat, whisking frequently, until mixture thickens. Remove from heat. Add gelatin, stirring until smooth. Let mixture cool to room temperature.

Arrange strawberries in prepared crust. Pour filling over strawberries, coating completely. Refrigerate until set, about 2 hours. Cover and refrigerate for up to 3 days.

The strawberries can be sliced and layered in a pattern before pouring over the filling. Smaller berries are easier to arrange than larger ones. They sometimes have hollow centers and may not be as sweet.

Peach Pie

Preheat oven to 350°.

In a large bowl, stir together peaches, sugar, tapioca flour, lemon zest, lemon juice, almond extract, cinnamon, salt, and nutmeg.

On a lightly floured surface, roll half of Buttermilk Pie Dough to a 12-inch circle. Transfer to a 9-inch deep-dish pie plate, pressing into bottom and up sides. Spoon peach filling into crust. Sprinkle butter over filling.

On a lightly floured surface, roll remaining dough to a 12-inch circle. Using a sharp knife or cookie cutter, cut out desired designs; discard scraps. Place crust over filling. Trim edges to extend 1/2-inch beyond edge of plate. Fold edges under, and crimp as desired. Brush dough with cream.

Bake until crust is golden brown and filling is bubbly, about 1 hour, loosely covering with foil to prevent excess browning, if necessary. Let cool completely on a wire rack.

MAKES 1 (9-INCH)
DEEP-DISH PIE

- **8 fresh peaches, peeled, pitted, and sliced (about 6 cups)**
- **3/4 cup sugar**
- **3 tablespoons tapioca flour**
- **1 teaspoon lemon zest**
- **1 tablespoon fresh lemon juice**
- **1/2 teaspoon almond extract**
- **1/2 teaspoon ground cinnamon**
- **1/4 teaspoon kosher salt**
- **1/8 teaspoon grated fresh nutmeg**
- **2 recipes Buttermilk Pie Dough (recipe on page 11)**
- **1 tablespoon unsalted butter, cubed**
- **1 tablespoon heavy whipping cream**

You can cut out shapes with small cookie cutters or freehand with a knife to vent and also make your pie look nice. Brushing the dough with cream or egg gives the pie a glossy shine on top.

Pear and Cranberry Slab Pie

4 cups plus 1 tablespoon all-purpose flour, divided

7 tablespoons sugar, divided

1 teaspoon salt

1¼ cups unsalted butter, divided

¼ cup all-vegetable shortening

12 to 14 tablespoons ice water

1 (6-ounce) bag dried sweetened cranberries

1 cup boiling water

6 firm ripe pears, peeled, cored, and sliced

2 tablespoons fresh lemon juice

½ teaspoon ground cinnamon

1 tablespoon whole milk

Garnish: sifted confectioners' sugar

In the work bowl of a food processor, pulse together 4 cups flour, 2 tablespoons sugar, and salt. Add 1 cup butter and shortening; pulse until mixture is crumbly. Transfer mixture to a large bowl. Add ice water, 1 tablespoon at a time, just until dry ingredients are moistened. On a lightly floured surface, gently knead dough 2 or 3 times until combined. Divide dough in half, and shape each half into a disk. Wrap in plastic wrap, and refrigerate for at least 1 hour.

In a medium bowl, combine cranberries and 1 cup boiling water. Cover and let stand for 30 minutes; drain. Return cranberries to bowl; add pears, 4 tablespoons sugar, lemon juice, cinnamon, and remaining 1 tablespoon flour, tossing to combine.

Preheat oven to 375°. Line a 15x10-inch rimmed baking sheet with parchment paper. On a lightly floured surface, roll half of dough into a 16x11-inch rectangle. Transfer to prepared pan, pressing into corners and letting excess dough extend over edges. Spoon pear mixture into prepared crust. Sprinkle with remaining ¼ cup butter.

On a lightly floured surface, roll remaining dough into a 15x10-inch rectangle. Cut dough lengthwise into 10 strips. Place 6 strips of dough lengthwise over pear mixture. Place remaining 4 strips of dough crosswise over pear mixture. Trim excess dough, pressing edges of strips into sides of dough. Brush with milk, and sprinkle with remaining 1 tablespoon sugar.

Bake until crust is golden brown and pears are tender, about 40 minutes. Let cool completely on a wire rack. Garnish with confectioners' sugar, if desired.

Strawberry-Rhubarb Pie

Preheat oven to 350°. On a lightly floured surface, roll Basic Pie Dough to a 12-inch circle. Transfer to a 9-inch pie plate, pressing into bottom and up sides. Fold edges under, and crimp as desired. Top with a piece of parchment paper, letting ends extend over edges of plate. Add pie weights.

Bake for 15 minutes. Carefully remove paper and weights. Bake until golden brown, about 10 minutes more. Let cool for 10 minutes. In a large saucepan, cook strawberries, rhubarb, and ½ cup sugar over medium heat, stirring occasionally, until berries are tender, about 8 minutes. Strain fruit through a fine-mesh sieve into a medium bowl; reserve 1 cup juice.

In another medium bowl, whisk together 1 cup reserved juice, tapioca flour, salt, and remaining ½ cup sugar. Add fruit to juice mixture, stirring gently to combine. Pour mixture into prepared crust.

Bake until crust is golden brown and filling is bubbly, 30 to 40 minutes, loosely covering with foil to prevent excess browning, if necessary. Transfer to a wire rack, and let cool to room temperature before serving. Garnish with Coconut Whipped Cream and toasted coconut, if desired.

COCONUT WHIPPED CREAM In a small saucepan, heat cream over medium heat until just beginning to bubble. Remove from heat; stir in coconut. Let steep for 10 minutes.

Strain cream through a fine-mesh sieve into an airtight container; discard coconut. Refrigerate until cold, about 2 hours. In a medium bowl, beat cream, confectioners' sugar, and salt with a mixer at medium speed until soft peaks form, about 3 minutes.

MAKES 1 (9-INCH) PIE

½ recipe Basic Pie Dough (recipe on page 10)
4 cups quartered fresh strawberries
1¼ cups chopped fresh rhubarb
1 cup sugar, divided
¼ cup tapioca flour
½ teaspoon salt
Garnish: Coconut Whipped Cream (recipe follows), toasted sweetened flaked coconut

COCONUT
WHIPPED CREAM
MAKES ABOUT 2 CUPS

1 cup heavy whipping cream
3/4 cup sweetened flaked coconut, toasted
¼ cup confectioners' sugar
¼ teaspoon kosher salt

Double-Apple Cranberry Pie

3 large Granny Smith apples (about 1¾ pounds), peeled, cored, and sliced

3 large Braeburn apples (about 1¾ pounds), peeled, cored, and sliced

½ cup dried cranberries

1 tablespoon fresh lemon juice

½ cup plus 2 teaspoons granulated sugar, divided

½ cup firmly packed light brown sugar

¼ cup all-purpose flour

1 teaspoon ground cinnamon

¼ teaspoon ground nutmeg

1 (14.1-ounce) package refrigerated piecrusts

2 tablespoons butter, cubed

1 large egg yolk, lightly beaten

Preheat oven to 425°.

In a large bowl, combine apples, cranberries, and lemon juice. In a small bowl, combine ½ cup granulated sugar, brown sugar, flour, cinnamon, and nutmeg. Pour over apple mixture, tossing gently.

On a lightly floured surface, roll half of dough to a 12-inch circle. Transfer to a 9-inch deep-dish pie plate, pressing into bottom and up sides. Pour apple mixture into prepared crust. (Filling will mound above rim of pie plate.) Sprinkle with butter.

On a lightly floured surface, roll remaining dough to ⅛-inch thickness; cut into 1-inch strips. Arrange strips in a lattice design over apple mixture. Fold edges under, and crimp as desired. Using a pastry brush, brush dough strips with egg yolk. Sprinkle with remaining 2 teaspoons granulated sugar.

Bake for 30 minutes; cover with foil, and bake until apples are softened, 30 to 45 minutes more. Let cool completely on a wire rack.

Peach-Blueberry Pie

Preheat oven to 425°.

On a lightly floured surface, roll half of dough to a 12-inch circle. Transfer to a 9-inch deep-dish pie plate, pressing into bottom and up sides.

In a large bowl, combine peaches, blueberries, sugar, flour, melted butter, and nutmeg, tossing gently to combine. Spoon fruit mixture into prepared crust.

On a lightly floured surface, roll remaining dough to an 11-inch circle. Place over filling. Fold edges under, and crimp as desired. Cut several 1-inch slits in top of dough to release steam.

Bake until crust is golden brown and filling is bubbly, 40 to 45 minutes, loosely covering with foil to prevent excess browning, if necessary. Let cool completely on a wire rack.

MAKES 1 (9-INCH)
DEEP-DISH PIE

1 (14.1-ounce) package refrigerated piecrusts
8 cups peeled and sliced fresh peaches
½ cup fresh blueberries
¼ cup sugar
2 tablespoons all-purpose flour
2 tablespoons butter, melted
¼ teaspoon unsalted nutmeg

Store fruit pies in the refrigerator after serving to keep them fresh. You can always heat leftover pie slices in the microwave to take away the chill. Or better still, add a dollop of ice cream or cream on top for an extra treat.

Cranberry-Apricot Crumble Pie

MAKES 1 (9-INCH)
DEEP-DISH PIE

1 (12-ounce) bag fresh cranberries, divided
1 cup granulated sugar
¼ cup plus 2 tablespoons all-purpose flour, divided
½ teaspoon apple pie spice
⅛ teaspoon salt
1 cup water
1 (6-ounce) bag dried apricots, chopped
6 tablespoons salted butter, softened and divided
½ (14.1-ounce) package refrigerated piecrusts
½ cup old-fashioned oats
½ cup firmly packed light brown sugar

Set aside 1 cup cranberries. In a medium saucepan, combine granulated sugar, 2 tablespoons flour, apple pie spice, salt, and remaining cranberries; stir in 1 cup water. Bring to a boil over medium-high heat. Reduce heat to medium-low; simmer until cranberries pop and mixture thickens, 5 to 7 minutes. Remove from heat; stir in 1 cup reserved cranberries, apricots, and 2 tablespoons butter.

Preheat oven to 375°. On a lightly floured surface, roll dough to a 12-inch circle. Transfer to a 9-inch deep-dish pie plate, pressing into bottom and up sides. Fold edges under, and crimp as desired.

In a medium bowl, combine oats, brown sugar, and remaining ¼ cup flour. Add remaining 4 tablespoons butter, combining with your fingertips until mixture is crumbly. Spoon cranberry mixture into prepared crust. Sprinkle with oat mixture.

Bake until crust is golden brown and filling is bubbly, 40 to 45 minutes, covering with foil during last 10 minutes of baking to prevent excess browning, if necessary. Let cool completely on a wire rack.

Blackberry Slab Pie

Make Basic Pie Dough, adding coffee extract and reserved vanilla bean seeds with ice water, if desired.

Line a 15x10-inch rimmed baking sheet with parchment paper.

On a lightly floured surface, roll half of dough into an 18x13-inch rectangle, about ⅛ inch thick. Transfer to prepared pan, pressing into corners and letting excess dough extend over edges. Refrigerate for 30 minutes.

Preheat oven to 350°.

In a large bowl, combine blackberries, ¾ cup sugar, tapioca flour, and salt. Spread mixture onto prepared crust.

On a lightly floured surface, roll remaining dough into a 16x11-inch rectangle, about ⅛-inch thick. Place over filling. Fold edges under, and crimp as desired. Cut several 1-inch slits in top of dough to release steam. Brush with cream, and sprinkle with remaining 2 tablespoons sugar.

Bake until crust is golden brown and filling is bubbly, 50 to 60 minutes. Let cool completely on a wire rack.

MAKES 1 (15X10-INCH) PIE

Basic Pie Dough (recipe on page 10)
1½ teaspoons coffee extract (optional)
1 vanilla bean, split lengthwise, seeds scraped and reserved (optional)
8 cups fresh blackberries
¾ cup plus 2 tablespoons sugar, divided
4 tablespoons tapioca flour
½ teaspoon kosher salt
2 tablespoons heavy whipping cream

Icebox
PIES

MAKE DESSERT AHEAD, AND BE READY
TO SERVE IT CHILLED WITH LAST-MINUTE
GARNISHES LIKE A DRIZZLE OF CARAMEL,
SPRINKLE OF MINT, OR SLICES OF FRUIT

Black Bottom Coconut Cream Pie

MAKES 1 (9-INCH) PIE

- ½ (14.1-ounce) package refrigerated piecrusts
- 1 (4-ounce) bar bittersweet chocolate, chopped
- ¾ teaspoon vanilla extract, divided
- 1½ cups heavy whipping cream, divided
- 1 tablespoon butter
- 2 cups whole milk
- 4 large egg yolks
- ½ cup granulated sugar
- ½ cup all-purpose flour
- ⅛ teaspoon salt
- 1¼ cups coconut milk, divided
- ¾ cup sweetened flaked coconut
- ¼ teaspoon coconut extract
- ⅓ cup confectioners' sugar
- Garnish: toasted sweetened flaked coconut

Preheat oven to 450°. Place dough in a 9-inch pie plate, pressing into bottom and up sides. Fold edges under, and crimp as desired. Prick bottom and sides of dough with a fork. Bake until light brown, about 10 minutes. Let cool completely.

In a medium bowl, place chopped chocolate and ¼ teaspoon vanilla. In a small saucepan, bring ½ cup cream and butter to a boil over medium heat. Pour hot cream mixture over chocolate; let stand for 30 seconds. Whisk until chocolate is melted and smooth. Let cool for 10 minutes. Pour chocolate mixture into prepared crust. Refrigerate for 30 minutes.

In a medium saucepan, bring milk to a simmer over medium heat. In a large bowl, whisk together egg yolks and granulated sugar until combined. Add flour, salt, and ¾ cup coconut milk, whisking until smooth. Slowly whisk hot milk into egg mixture. Return egg mixture to saucepan. Cook, whisking constantly, until bubbly, about 3 minutes. Let cook for 1 minute, whisking until thickened. Remove from heat; stir in coconut, coconut extract, and remaining ½ teaspoon vanilla.

Place saucepan in a large bowl of ice. Let stand, stirring occasionally, until coconut mixture has cooled to room temperature, about 30 minutes. Spread coconut mixture over chocolate layer in prepared crust. Place a piece of plastic wrap directly on surface of filling. Refrigerate until chilled, about 4 hours. In a medium bowl, beat confectioners' sugar, remaining 1 cup cream, and remaining ½ cup coconut milk with a mixer at high speed just until stiff peaks form. Spread whipped cream mixture over filling. Garnish with coconut, if desired.

Blackberry Lemonade Pie

In the work bowl of a food processor, pulse cookies until finely ground. Add melted butter, pulsing to combine. Using a measuring cup, press mixture into bottom and up sides of a 9-inch pie plate. Freeze for 10 minutes.

In a large bowl, beat cream cheese with a mixer at high speed until smooth. Add condensed milk; beat for 1 minute. Add lemon zest and lemon juice; beat 1 minute more. Pour into prepared crust. Spoon preserves over filling; swirl gently using a knife. Cover and refrigerate overnight.

MAKES 1 (9-INCH) PIE

12 cream-filled vanilla sandwich cookies*
½ cup melted butter
2 (8-ounce) packages cream cheese, softened
1 (14-ounce) can sweetened condensed milk
1 teaspoon lemon zest
¾ cup fresh lemon juice
¼ cup blackberry preserves, melted and cooled

We used Golden Oreos.

Fresh blackberries tend to be tart in flavor. The fruit changes from green to red, and finally to dark blue before it is ready to pick.

Cherry Limeade Icebox Pie

Makes 1 (9-inch) pie

½ **(5-ounce) package sugar ice cream cones (about 8 cones)**
½ **cup butter, melted**
1 **(3-ounce) box black cherry gelatin**
1 **cup boiling water**
¼ **cup maraschino cherry juice (from jar)**
½ **cup fresh lime juice**
1 **(14-ounce) can sweetened condensed milk**
Garnish: whipped topping, maraschino cherries, lime slices

In the work bowl of a food processor, pulse cones until coarsely ground. Add melted butter, pulsing to combine. Using a measuring cup, press mixture into bottom and up sides of a 9-inch pie plate. Freeze for 10 minutes.

In a medium bowl, stir together gelatin and 1 cup boiling water until gelatin dissolves. Stir in cherry juice; refrigerate for 30 minutes.

In a small bowl, stir together lime zest, lime juice, and condensed milk; stir into cherry mixture. Pour into prepared crust. Cover and refrigerate overnight. Garnish with whipped topping, cherries, and lime slices, if desired.

A favorite beverage for me was the cherry limeade at a local quick mart. Who can resist these two flavors combined? Simply yummy!

Icebox Mocha Tart

Remove sides from an 8½-inch round springform pan. Line pan with wax paper, leaving an overhang; lock sides onto bottom, firmly securing paper. Spray with cooking spray.

In the work bowl of a food processor, process chocolate wafer cookies until finely ground. In a small bowl, combine cookie crumbs and granulated sugar. Stir in melted butter. Using a measuring cup, press mixture into bottom of prepared pan. Refrigerate for 15 minutes.

Place chopped chocolate in a small microwave-safe bowl. Microwave on high in 30-second intervals, stirring between each, until chocolate is melted and smooth (about 1½ minutes total).

In a small bowl, combine 2 tablespoons water and espresso powder, stirring until dissolved.

In a large bowl, beat cream cheese and mascarpone cheese with a mixer at medium speed until smooth. Add melted chocolate and espresso mixture, beating until well combined. Gradually beat in confectioners' sugar until smooth. Spoon chocolate mixture into prepared pan. Refrigerate for 4 hours.

Just before serving, release sides of pan. Carefully transfer tart to a serving platter. Garnish with chocolate-covered espresso beans, if desired.

MAKES 1 (8½-INCH) PIE

1 (9-ounce) box chocolate wafer cookies
3 tablespoons granulated sugar
½ cup butter, melted
2 (4-ounce) bars semisweet chocolate, chopped
2 tablespoons water
1 tablespoon espresso powder
2 (8-ounce) packages cream cheese, softened
2 (8-ounce) containers mascarpone cheese
1 cup confectioners' sugar
Garnish: chopped chocolate-covered espresso beans

Strawberry Chiffon Pie

MAKES 1 (9-INCH) PIE

2 cups graham cracker crumbs
½ cup finely ground pistachios
¼ cup sugar
½ teaspoon kosher salt
6 tablespoons unsalted butter, melted
¾ cup boiling water
1 (3-ounce) box strawberry gelatin
¼ cup small ice cubes
1 teaspoon lemon zest
2 tablespoons fresh lemon juice
1 (12-ounce) container frozen whipped topping, thawed
2 cups finely chopped strawberries

Preheat oven to 350°.

In the work bowl of a food processor, pulse together graham cracker crumbs, pistachios, sugar, and salt. With processor running, slowly add melted butter until well combined. Using a measuring cup, press mixture into bottom and up sides of a 9-inch deep-dish pie plate.

Bake until crust is golden brown, 15 to 20 minutes. Let cool completely.

In a small bowl, stir together ¾ cup boiling water and gelatin until completely dissolved, about 2 minutes. Add ice, and stir until completely melted. Stir in lemon zest and lemon juice. Whisk whipped topping into gelatin mixture until well combined. Gently fold in chopped strawberries.

Cover and refrigerate until mixture thickens, about 1 hour. Spoon into prepared crust. Freeze until firm, about 2 hours. Serve cold.

Chiffon sounds so elegant! The original recipe, invented by Monroe Strause in 1926, called for beaten egg whites to be folded into a thickened cornstarch liquid.

Pineapple-Coconut Cream Pie

In a medium bowl, stir together cookie crumbs and melted butter. Using a measuring cup, press mixture into bottom and up sides of a 9-inch pie plate. Freeze for 10 minutes.

In a medium bowl, whisk together cream of coconut and milk until smooth. Whisk in pudding mix until smooth. Stir in pineapple and sour cream; pour into prepared crust. Cover and refrigerate overnight. Garnish with whipped topping, pineapple, and coconut, if desired.

MAKES 1 (9-INCH) PIE

1½ cups crushed coconut
    cookies*
½ cup butter, melted
1 (15-ounce) can cream
    of coconut
⅓ cup whole milk
1 (3.4-ounce) box coconut
    cream instant pudding
    and pie filling
1 (8-ounce) can crushed
    pineapple
1 (8-ounce) container sour
    cream
Garnish: whipped topping,
    chopped pineapple,
    toasted coconut

*We used Archway.

Cookie crumbs make terrific pie shell crusts with the simple addition of butter or a binder. It is so quick and easy to prepare.

Frozen Peppermint Mousse Pie

1²/₃ cups finely ground chocolate wafer cookies (about 24 cookies)
¼ cup granulated sugar
¼ cup butter, melted
1 tablespoon all-purpose flour
⅛ teaspoon salt
1 cup whole milk
1 large egg yolk
¼ cup cream cheese, softened and cubed
½ (4-ounce) bar white chocolate, finely chopped
2 tablespoons white crème de menthe, or to taste
1 to 2 drops red food coloring (optional)
1 cup heavy whipping cream
¼ cup confectioners' sugar
Garnish: sweetened whipped cream, crushed peppermints

Spray a 9-inch pie plate with cooking spray.

In a medium bowl, combine cookie crumbs and granulated sugar. Drizzle with melted butter, tossing with a fork until moistened. Using a measuring cup, press mixture into bottom and up sides of prepared plate. Freeze for 30 minutes.

In a medium saucepan, combine flour and salt; whisk in milk. Bring to a boil over medium heat, stirring constantly. Cook, stirring constantly, until thickened and bubbly, about 2 minutes. Remove from heat.

Place egg yolk in a medium bowl. Slowly stir in half of hot milk mixture. Stir egg yolk mixture into remaining hot milk mixture in saucepan. Cook over medium-low heat, stirring constantly, until thickened and bubbly, about 2 minutes. Remove from heat. Add cream cheese and white chocolate; stir until melted and smooth. Stir in crème de menthe and food coloring (if using). Spoon into a bowl; cover and refrigerate until chilled, about 1 hour.

In a medium bowl, beat cream and confectioners' sugar with a mixer at high speed until stiff peaks form; gently fold into cream cheese mixture. Spread into prepared crust. Freeze until firm, 4 to 5 hours. Remove from freezer 10 minutes before serving. Garnish with whipped cream and peppermints, if desired.

Strawberry Frozen Yogurt Pie

Spray a 10-inch springform pan with baking spray with flour; line with parchment paper, and spray pan again.

In a large bowl, stir together graham cracker crumbs, pretzels, and ½ cup granulated sugar. Add melted butter, stirring to combine. Using a measuring cup, press mixture into bottom of prepared pan; freeze for 30 minutes.

In the work bowl of a food processor, combine strawberries and remaining ½ cup granulated sugar; pulse until smooth.

In a medium bowl, beat half of cream cheese with a mixer at high speed until creamy, about 3 minutes. Reduce mixer speed to medium; add ½ cup yogurt and ¼ cup confectioners' sugar, beating until smooth. Add strawberry mixture to cream cheese mixture, beating to combine. Add 1 container whipped topping, and beat until smooth. Spoon mixture onto prepared crust, and spread until smooth. Cover and freeze for 2 hours.

In a medium bowl, beat remaining cream cheese and remaining ¼ cup confectioners' sugar with a mixer at high speed until creamy. In another medium bowl, beat pudding mix, cream, vanilla, and remaining 1 cup yogurt with a mixer at medium-high speed until thick and creamy, about 2 minutes. Add pudding mixture to cream cheese mixture, beating to combine. Add remaining container whipped topping, and beat until combined.

Spoon mixture over strawberry layer. Cover and freeze for at least 4 hours or overnight. Garnish with strawberries and blueberries, if desired. Cover and freeze for up to 1 week.

MAKES 1 (10-INCH) PIE

1 cup graham cracker crumbs
1 cup ground pretzels
1 cup granulated sugar, divided
½ cup butter, melted
2 cups chopped fresh strawberries
1 (8-ounce) package cream cheese, softened and divided
1½ cups vanilla yogurt, divided
½ cup confectioners' sugar, divided
2 (8-ounce) containers frozen whipped topping, thawed and divided
1 (3.4-ounce) box white chocolate instant pudding mix
1 cup heavy whipping cream
1 teaspoon vanilla extract
Garnish: fresh strawberries, fresh blueberries

Whipped Cream Pie with Salted Caramel

1½ **cups graham cracker crumbs**
½ **cup butter, melted**
1 **(0.25-ounce) envelope unflavored gelatin**
2 **tablespoons cold water**
3 **cups heavy whipping cream, divided**
¼ **cup firmly packed light brown sugar**
1 **teaspoon vanilla extract**
Garnish: prepared caramel sauce, flaked sea salt

In a medium bowl, stir together graham cracker crumbs and melted butter. Using a measuring cup, press mixture into bottom and up sides of a 9-inch pie plate. Freeze for 10 minutes.

In a small bowl, stir together gelatin and 2 tablespoons cold water; let stand for 1 minute. Microwave ½ cup cream for 45 seconds; pour over gelatin, whisking until gelatin dissolves. Refrigerate for 5 minutes.

In a large bowl, beat brown sugar, vanilla, and remaining 2½ cups cream with a mixer at medium speed until fluffy. Gradually add gelatin mixture, beating until medium peaks form. Spoon into prepared crust. Refrigerate overnight. Garnish with caramel sauce and sea salt, if desired.

I have found more uses for gelatin, like sprinkling over fresh fruit to add flavor and sweetness. I have also prepared some great party punches using a variety of gelatin flavors.

Chocolate-Buttermilk Icebox Pie

Preheat oven to 325°.

In a medium bowl, stir together graham cracker crumbs, pecans, brown sugar, and salt. Add melted butter, stirring to combine. Using a measuring cup, press mixture into bottom and up sides of a 9-inch deep-dish pie plate or removable-bottom tart pan.

Bake for 8 minutes. Remove from oven, and let cool completely.

In a large bowl, whisk together pudding mix, buttermilk, and vanilla until thickened, about 2 minutes. Whisk in whipped topping and ground chocolate. Pour mixture into prepared crust. Cover and freeze for at least 8 hours or overnight.

Remove from freezer, and refrigerate until serving. Cover and refrigerate for up to 1 week.

MAKES 1 (9-INCH)
DEEP-DISH PIE

- 1 cup chocolate graham cracker crumbs
- 1 (15-ounce) package glazed pecans, chopped
- ¼ cup firmly packed light brown sugar
- ¼ teaspoon salt
- 6 tablespoons butter, melted
- 2 (3.9-ounce) boxes chocolate instant pudding and pie filling
- 2¾ cups whole buttermilk
- 1 teaspoon vanilla extract
- 1 (8-ounce) container frozen whipped topping, thawed
- 1 cup sweetened ground chocolate

Peaches and Cream Icebox Pie

1½ cups gingersnap cookie crumbs (about 30 cookies)

½ cup butter, melted

1 (3.4-ounce) box cheesecake instant pudding and pie filling

1½ cups whole milk

1 (8-ounce) container sour cream

½ cup peach preserves, divided

½ cup chopped fresh peaches

Sweetened whipped cream

Garnish: fresh mint leaves

In a medium bowl, stir together cookie crumbs and melted butter. Using a measuring cup, press mixture into bottom and up sides of a 9-inch pie plate. Freeze for 10 minutes.

Prepare pudding mix according to package directions, reducing milk to 1½ cups. Fold in sour cream. Pour into prepared crust; refrigerate for 10 minutes.

Spoon ¼ cup peach preserves over filling; swirl gently with a knife. In a small bowl, stir together peaches and remaining ¼ cup preserves. Top pie with whipped cream; spoon peach mixture over top. Garnish with mint, if desired.

Tarts

GLAZED AND EMBELLISHED
WITH FRUITS AND CREAM,
FREESTANDING TARTS AND
TARTLETS MAKE GRAND
IMPRESSIONS

Buttermilk Blueberry Tart

MAKES 1 (9-INCH) TART

½ (14.1-ounce) package
    refrigerated piecrusts
1 cup fresh blueberries
1½ cups sugar
½ cup unsalted butter,
    melted
½ cup whole buttermilk
3 large eggs
1 tablespoon all-purpose
    flour
1 teaspoon ground
    allspice
Molasses Swirl Whipped
    Cream (recipe
    follows)

MOLASSES SWIRL
WHIPPED CREAM
MAKES 3 CUPS

1 cup heavy whipping
    cream
2 tablespoons
    confectioners' sugar
1 teaspoon vanilla extract
1 tablespoon molasses

Preheat oven to 350°.

On a lightly floured surface, roll dough to a 12-inch circle.
Transfer to a 9-inch removable-bottom tart, pressing into
bottom and up sides. Sprinkle with blueberries.

In a medium bowl, whisk together sugar, melted butter,
buttermilk, eggs, flour, and allspice until combined.
Pour mixture over blueberries.

Bake until center is set, about 1 hour. Let cool completely
on a wire rack. Gently remove from pan. Serve with
Molasses Swirl Whipped Cream.

MOLASSES SWIRL WHIPPED CREAM In a medium bowl,
beat cream, confectioners' sugar, and vanilla with a mixer
at medium speed until stiff peaks form. Using a spoon,
drizzle molasses over cream mixture. Using a wooden
pick, swirl molasses into cream mixture.

Easy Apple-Ginger Tart

Preheat oven to 450°.

Place dough in a 9-inch removable-bottom tart pan, pressing into bottom and up sides.

In a large bowl, combine apple slices, cornstarch, and sugar, tossing gently to coat. Arrange apple slices in a single layer on dough.

Bake until crust is lightly golden, 15 to 20 minutes. Let cool in pan for 10 minutes. Sprinkle ginger over apples.

In a small microwave-safe bowl, place marmalade. Microwave on high until melted, about 30 seconds. Brush over apples. Sprinkle with zest.

MAKES 1 (9-INCH) TART

½ **(14.1-ounce) package refrigerated piecrusts**
1½ **large Braeburn apples, cored and thinly sliced**
1½ **large Granny Smith apples, cored and thinly sliced**
1 **tablespoon plus 1 teaspoon cornstarch**
1 **tablespoon sugar**
2 **tablespoons chopped crystallized ginger**
⅓ **cup orange marmalade**
1 **teaspoon orange zest**

Keeping the peel gives more interest to your apple tart. By simply alternating two different apples, you will have a delicious and irresistible dessert.

Hazelnut Truffle Tart

MAKES 1 (9-INCH) TART

2 cups crushed chocolate
    wafer cookies
½ cup finely chopped
    hazelnuts
6 tablespoons butter, melted
3 tablespoons sugar
1 large egg white, lightly
    beaten
½ cup heavy whipping cream
4 (4-ounce) bars semisweet
    chocolate, chopped
½ cup chocolate-hazelnut
    spread*
Garnish: chopped hazelnuts

We used Nutella.

Preheat oven to 350°.

In a small bowl, stir together crushed cookies, hazelnuts, melted butter, sugar, and egg white. Using a measuring cup, press mixture into bottom and up sides of a 9-inch removable-bottom tart pan. Place pan on a baking sheet.

Bake for 10 minutes. Let cool completely.

In a medium microwave-safe bowl, combine cream and chocolate. Microwave on high in 30-second intervals, stirring between each, until chocolate is melted and smooth (about 2 minutes total). Add chocolate-hazelnut spread, stirring until smooth. Spoon chocolate mixture into prepared crust. Refrigerate until set, about 2 hours. Garnish with hazelnuts, if desired.

Pie servers are essential for cutting and serving pie. I like to use two that I have collected—one is thin and pointed on the end for cutting through thick pies, and the other has a rounded blade to make serving slices a bit easier.

Recipe TIP

To make sugared rosemary
sprigs, dip sprigs in water,
shaking off excess. Lightly
dredge in sugar; repeat, if
necessary. Use immediately.

Cranberry Swirl Cheesecake Tart

Preheat oven to 350°. Spray an 11-inch removable-bottom tart pan with cooking spray. In the work bowl of a food processor, pulse together cookies and butter until finely ground, about 8 times. Using a measuring cup, press mixture into bottom and up sides of prepared pan.

Bake for 8 minutes. Let cool for 30 minutes. In a small saucepan, combine cranberries, 3 tablespoons water, lemon juice, 2 tablespoons sugar, and corn syrup; bring to a boil over medium-high heat. Reduce heat to medium-low; simmer until cranberries pop and mixture thickens, about 5 minutes. Remove from heat; let cool for 15 minutes, stirring occasionally.

Pour cranberry mixture into the container of a blender. Process until smooth, stopping occasionally to scrape sides of container. Pour cranberry mixture into a medium bowl. In a large bowl, beat cream cheese, flour, and remaining 2/3 cup sugar with a mixer at medium speed until smooth, stopping to scrape sides of bowl. Add sour cream, vanilla, and zest, beating until combined. Add eggs, one at a time, beating well after each addition. Spread cream cheese mixture into prepared crust.

Drop cranberry mixture by teaspoonfuls over cream cheese mixture. (If cranberry mixture has thickened while cooling, stir in just enough water to thin mixture before dropping onto cream cheese mixture.) Lightly swirl cranberry mixture using a wooden pick. Gently place tart on a rimmed baking sheet. Bake until set, 25 to 30 minutes. Remove from baking sheet. Let cool on a wire rack for 30 minutes. Lightly cover and refrigerate until chilled, about 3 hours. Garnish with sugared cranberries and sugared rosemary sprigs, if desired.

MAKES 1 (11-INCH) TART

- **1 (9-ounce) box chocolate wafer cookies***
- **6 tablespoons cold unsalted butter, cubed**
- **1 cup fresh or frozen cranberries, thawed**
- **3 tablespoons water**
- **2 tablespoons fresh lemon juice**
- **2/3 cup plus 2 tablespoons sugar, divided**
- **2 tablespoons light corn syrup**
- **2 (8-ounce) packages cream cheese, softened**
- **1 tablespoon all-purpose flour**
- **1 (8-ounce) container sour cream**
- **1 teaspoon vanilla extract**
- **1/2 teaspoon lemon zest**
- **2 large eggs**
- **Garnish: sugared cranberries, sugared rosemary sprigs (see Recipe Tip)**

We used Famous Chocolate Wafers.

White Chocolate and Toasted Nut Tart

1 (12-ounce) jar prepared caramel topping, divided

Best Tart Shell (recipe follows)

3 (4-ounce) bars white chocolate, chopped

¼ cup plus 3 tablespoons heavy whipping cream

¼ cup butter

2 tablespoons light corn syrup

1 (11.5-ounce) can mixed nuts, toasted

¼ cup walnuts, toasted

¼ cup macadamia nuts, toasted

BEST TART SHELL
Makes 1 (11x9-inch) tart shell

1½ cups all-purpose flour

¼ cup confectioners' sugar

¼ teaspoon salt

½ cup unsalted butter, softened

1 large egg yolk

1 tablespoon heavy whipping cream

Pour half of prepared caramel topping into prepared Best Tart Shell, spreading to cover entire surface. Refrigerate for 30 minutes.

Place white chocolate in a medium bowl. In a medium saucepan, bring cream, butter, and corn syrup to a boil over high heat. Pour cream mixture over chopped chocolate, whisking until melted and smooth. Pour chocolate mixture over caramel in prepared tart shell. Refrigerate until set, about 2 hours.

In a medium bowl, combine nuts and remaining caramel sauce. Gently spoon nut mixture on top of tart. Remove sides of tart pan before serving. Store, covered, at room temperature for up to 2 days.

BEST TART SHELL In the work bowl of a food processor, pulse together flour, confectioners' sugar, and salt until combined. Add butter, egg yolk, and cream, pulsing until mixture comes together. Turn out dough, and shape into a disk. Wrap in plastic wrap, and refrigerate for 2 hours.

Preheat oven to 350°.

On a lightly floured surface, roll dough into a 13x11-inch rectangle, ¼-inch thick. Transfer to an 11x9-inch tart pan, pressing into bottom and up sides. Top with a piece of parchment paper, letting ends extend over edges of pan. Add pie weights.

Bake until golden brown, about 30 minutes. Carefully remove paper and weights. Let cool for 30 minutes.

Cranberry-Caramel Tart

Preheat oven to 350°.

CRUST In the work bowl of a food processor, combine flour, confectioners' sugar, pecans, and salt. Pulse until finely ground. With processor running, slowly add butter; process just until dough comes together. Press dough into bottom and up sides of a 9-inch removable-bottom tart pan. Freeze for 10 minutes.

Prick bottom and sides of dough with a fork. Top with a piece of parchment paper, letting ends extend over edges of pan. Add pie weights.

Bake for 20 minutes. Carefully remove paper and weights. Bake until lightly browned, about 5 minutes more. Let cool on a wire rack.

FILLING In a 10-inch skillet, sprinkle sugar in an even layer. Cook over medium heat until sugar dissolves and turns an amber color, about 10 minutes. (Do not stir.) Remove from heat. Carefully stir in butter and warm cream, whisking until combined. Stir in pecans, cranberries, and salt. Spoon mixture into prepared crust.

Bake until bubbly, 20 to 25 minutes. Let cool to room temperature. Refrigerate for at least 30 minutes before slicing.

MAKES 1 (9-INCH) TART

CRUST
3/4 cup all-purpose flour
1/4 cup plus 2 tablespoons
    confectioners' sugar
1/4 cup toasted pecans
1/4 teaspoon kosher salt
1/3 cup unsalted butter,
    softened and cubed

FILLING
1 cup sugar
1/2 cup unsalted butter,
    softened
1 cup heavy whipping
    cream, warmed
2 cups chopped pecans
2 cups frozen cranberries
1/4 teaspoon kosher salt

Lime Chess Tart

2 cups granulated sugar
2 tablespoons plain yellow
    cornmeal
1½ tablespoons all-purpose flour
6 large eggs
1 tablespoon lime zest
½ cup fresh lime juice
6 tablespoons unsalted
    butter, melted
¼ cup whole milk
Shortbread Pastry Shell
    (recipe follows)
Garnish: Candied Limes (recipe
    follows), confectioners'
    sugar, whipped topping

SHORTBREAD PASTRY SHELL
Makes 1 (10-inch) deep-dish
tart shell

2¼ cups all-purpose flour
½ cup sugar
¼ teaspoon salt
¾ cup cold unsalted butter, cubed
1 large egg yolk

CANDIED LIMES
Makes about 12

1 cup water
1 cup sugar
1 tablespoon light corn syrup
4 limes, cut into ⅛-inch-thick
    slices

Preheat oven to 350°. In a large bowl, whisk together granulated sugar, cornmeal, and flour. Add eggs, one at a time, whisking well after each addition. Whisk in lime zest, lime juice, melted butter, and milk until smooth. Pour mixture into prepared Shortbread Pastry Shell.

Bake for 20 minutes. Cover with foil, and bake until center is set, 20 to 25 minutes more. Let cool for 2 hours before cutting. Garnish with Candied Limes, confectioners' sugar, and whipped topping, if desired.

SHORTBREAD PASTRY SHELL Preheat oven to 350°. Spray a 10-inch deep-dish removable-bottom tart pan with baking spray with flour.

In the work bowl of a food processor, pulse together flour, sugar, and salt. With processor running, add butter and egg yolk, and process until mixture is crumbly. Press mixture into bottom and up sides of prepared pan. Bake until lightly browned, about 15 minutes. Let cool for 15 minutes.

CANDIED LIMES In a large skillet, whisk together 1 cup water, sugar, and corn syrup. Heat over medium heat until sugar dissolves. Add lime slices, and bring to a boil. Cook for 3 minutes per side.

Transfer lime rounds to a wire rack, and let cool to room temperature. Do not stack candied limes before use.

Pear-Almond Crostata

CRUST In the work bowl of a food processor, pulse together flour, sugar, and salt. Add butter, and pulse until mixture is crumbly. Transfer mixture to a large bowl. Sprinkle with ice water, 1 tablespoon at a time, tossing with a fork just until dry ingredients are moistened.

Turn out dough onto a lightly floured surface, and knead just until combined, 2 to 3 times. Shape dough into a disk. Wrap in plastic wrap, and refrigerate for 30 minutes.

Preheat oven to 375°. Line a baking sheet with parchment paper.

On a lightly floured surface, roll dough to a 12-inch circle. Transfer to prepared pan.

FILLING Sprinkle almond paste over dough, leaving a 2-inch border.

In a large bowl, combine pears, granulated sugar, flour, ginger, and salt. Sprinkle lemon juice over pears, tossing to combine. Arrange pear mixture over almond paste. Gently fold edges of dough over filling. (Dough will not completely cover filling.)

In a small bowl, whisk together egg and 1 teaspoon water. Brush edges of dough with egg wash, and sprinkle with turbinado sugar.

Bake until crust is golden brown and filling is bubbly, about 40 minutes. Let cool for 20 minutes. Garnish with honey and almonds, if desired.

MAKES ABOUT 6 SERVINGS

CRUST
1⅓ cups all-purpose flour
2 tablespoons sugar
½ teaspoon salt
½ cup cold unsalted butter, cubed
5 to 6 tablespoons ice water

FILLING
2 tablespoons almond paste, crumbled
5 medium ripe Bartlett pears, peeled, cored, and sliced (about 2 pounds)
2 tablespoons granulated sugar
2 teaspoons all-purpose flour
½ teaspoon ground ginger
⅛ teaspoon salt
1 tablespoon fresh lemon juice
1 large egg
1 teaspoon water
2 teaspoons turbinado sugar
Garnish: honey, toasted sliced almonds

Plum Tart

2½ cups finely ground vanilla wafers
½ cup finely ground toasted walnuts
¼ cup granulated sugar
¼ teaspoon salt
5 tablespoons unsalted butter, melted
2 cups heavy whipping cream
½ cup confectioners' sugar
½ teaspoon ground cardamom
4 cups sliced plums (about 7 to 8 plums)

Preheat oven to 350°.

In the work bowl of a food processor, pulse together vanilla wafers, walnuts, granulated sugar, and salt. With processor running, slowly add melted butter until mixture is well combined. Using a measuring cup, press mixture into bottom and up sides of an 11x8-inch removable-bottom tart pan.

Bake until crust is golden, 15 to 20 minutes. Let cool completely.

In a large bowl, beat cream, confectioners' sugar, and cardamom with a mixer at medium-high speed until stiff peaks form. Spoon cream mixture into prepared crust. Place rows of sliced plums on top of cream mixture. Serve immediately, or refrigerate until ready to serve.

A tart pan ring can be removed easily by placing a wide can on the counter and setting the cooled tart pan on top. Hold the pan ring and gently pull it downward.

Pumpkin Spice Tartlets

In a medium bowl, beat cream cheese with a mixer at high speed until smooth, about 3 minutes. Add sugar; beat until fluffy. Add pumpkin, egg, evaporated milk, melted butter, allspice, cloves, ginger, nutmeg, cardamom, and cinnamon, beating until combined. Divide mixture among prepared Chocolate Shortbread Tartlet Shells.

Bake until set, about 15 minutes. Let cool for 15 minutes. To serve, remove bottoms and sides of tart pans. Garnish with chocolate curls, if desired.

CHOCOLATE SHORTBREAD TARTLET SHELLS

In the work bowl of a food processor, combine flour, confectioners' sugar, cocoa, cinnamon, and salt. Pulse until combined. Add butter and vanilla, pulsing until smooth. Turn out dough, and shape into a disk. Wrap in plastic wrap, and refrigerate for 2 hours.

Preheat oven to 350°.

On a lightly floured surface, roll dough to ¼-inch thickness. Using a 6½-inch round cutter, cut dough. Press dough into bottom and up sides of 6 (4½-inch) removable-bottom tart pans. Line shells with parchment paper, letting ends extend over edges of crusts. Add pie weights.

Bake for 15 minutes. Carefully remove paper and weights. Let cool for 15 minutes.

MAKES 6 (4½-INCH) TARTS

3 ounces cream cheese, softened
½ cup sugar
1 cup canned pumpkin
1 large egg
1 (5-ounce) can evaporated milk
2 tablespoons butter, melted
¼ teaspoon ground allspice
¼ teaspoon ground cloves
¼ teaspoon ground ginger
¼ teaspoon ground nutmeg
⅛ teaspoon ground cardamom
⅛ teaspoon ground cinnamon
Chocolate Shortbread Tartlet Shells (recipe follows)
Garnish: chocolate curls

CHOCOLATE SHORTBREAD
TARTLET SHELLS
MAKES 6 (4½-INCH) TART SHELLS

1 cup all-purpose flour
½ cup plus 2 tablespoons confectioners' sugar
¼ cup plus 1 tablespoon unsweetened cocoa powder
½ teaspoon ground cinnamon
¼ teaspoon salt
¾ cup butter, softened
½ teaspoon vanilla extract

White Chocolate Fruit Tart

MAKES 1 (9-INCH) TART

½ **(14.1-ounce) package refrigerated piecrusts**
1 **(8-ounce) package cream cheese, softened**
½ **cup confectioners' sugar**
½ **cup sour cream**
1 **(3.3-ounce) box white chocolate instant pudding and pie filling**
1 **cup heavy whipping cream**
¼ **cup whole milk**
4 **kiwis, peeled and quartered**
½ **(1-pound) container fresh strawberries, halved**
1 **pint fresh blueberries**
1 **pint fresh raspberries**
2 **tablespoons apricot preserves, melted**

Preheat oven to 450°.

On a lightly floured surface, roll dough to a 12-inch circle. Transfer to a 9-inch removable-bottom tart pan, pressing into bottom and up sides. Top with a piece of parchment paper, letting ends extend over edges of pan. Add pie weights.

Bake until lightly browned, 12 to 15 minutes. Carefully remove paper and weights. Let cool completely.

In a medium bowl, beat cream cheese, confectioners' sugar, sour cream, and pudding mix with a mixer at medium speed until smooth. Add cream and milk, beating until smooth. Spoon cream cheese mixture into prepared crust. Cover and refrigerate for at least 1 hour.

Top with kiwis, strawberries, blueberries, and raspberries. Brush fruit with apricot preserves.

Sometimes I use fruit I have on hand for a topping or garnish, rather than purchasing. A variety of berry sizes and shapes just make the dessert more desirable to your guests. Glazing fruit with preserves or honey adds shine.

Tiny
PIES

INDIVIDUAL SERVINGS OR HANDHELD,
THESE SMALL PIES ARE EASY
TO CARRY ALONG FOR TRAVEL
OR DINING OUTDOORS

Blueberry Hand Pies

Makes 12

Puff Pastry-Style Pie Dough (recipe follows)
1 cup fresh blueberries
⅓ cup granulated sugar
1 tablespoon all-purpose flour
½ teaspoon lemon zest
1 tablespoon fresh lemon juice
⅛ teaspoon kosher salt
⅛ teaspoon ground cardamom
⅛ teaspoon ground cinnamon
1 large egg, lightly beaten
1 tablespoon coarse sugar

PUFF PASTRY-STYLE
PIE DOUGH
Makes dough for
12 hand pies

2 cups all-purpose flour
½ teaspoon kosher salt
½ teaspoon baking powder
1 cup cold unsalted butter, cubed
½ cup whole buttermilk, chilled

Preheat oven to 425°. Line 2 baking sheets with parchment paper. On a lightly floured surface, roll Puff Pastry-Style Pie Dough into a 15-inch square. Using a 3-inch round cutter, cut 24 rounds, rerolling scraps as necessary. Place 6 dough rounds on each prepared pan; reserve remaining 12 dough rounds.

In a medium bowl, stir together blueberries, granulated sugar, flour, lemon zest, lemon juice, salt, cardamom, and cinnamon.

Place a heaping tablespoon of blueberry mixture onto center of each round on prepared pans. Brush edges of dough with egg. Place reserved rounds over blueberry mixture, and crimp edges with a fork to seal. Brush tops with egg, and sprinkle with coarse sugar. Cut 3 small vents in tops of dough to release steam.

Bake until golden brown, 15 to 18 minutes. Let cool slightly before serving.

PUFF PASTRY-STYLE PIE DOUGH In a large bowl, whisk together flour, salt, and baking powder. Using a pastry blender, cut in butter until mixture is crumbly. Add buttermilk, stirring until well combined.

Turn out dough onto a lightly floured surface, kneading briefly until dough comes together. Shape dough into a log. Roll dough into a 10x8-inch rectangle. Lightly flour both sides, and fold rectangle into thirds, letter-style. Rotate dough 90 degrees, and roll into another 10x8-inch rectangle. Lightly flour both sides, fold into thirds, and cover tightly with plastic wrap. Refrigerate for at least 30 minutes, or place in a heavy-duty resealable plastic bag, and freeze for up to 3 months.

Fried Cherry-Walnut Pies

In a medium saucepan, stir together granulated sugar, corn syrup, melted butter, and eggs. Stir in walnuts, vanilla, and salt. Bring to a boil over medium heat; reduce heat, and simmer for 10 minutes. Stir in cherries. Remove from heat, and let cool for 20 minutes.

On a lightly floured surface, roll each piecrust to ⅛-inch thickness. Using a 4-inch round cutter, cut dough, rerolling scraps as necessary. Brush edges of dough with egg yolk. Place a heaping tablespoon of walnut mixture onto center of each round. Fold dough over filling, and press edges to seal.

In a large Dutch oven, pour oil to a depth of 5 inches. Heat over medium heat until a deep-fry thermometer registers 350°. Fry pies, in batches, until lightly browned, about 1 minute per side. Let drain on paper towels. Garnish with confectioners' sugar, if desired.

MAKES ABOUT 24

1 cup granulated sugar
⅔ cup light corn syrup
⅓ cup butter, melted
2 large eggs
1½ cups chopped walnuts
1 teaspoon vanilla extract
⅛ teaspoon salt
¼ cup finely chopped
    dried cherries
2 (14.1-ounce) packages
    refrigerated piecrusts
1 large egg yolk, lightly
    beaten
Vegetable oil, for frying
Garnish: confectioners'
    sugar

I was so fortunate to watch my grandmother dry all sorts of fresh fruit during summer visits in the country. Setting the oven at a low temperature, she would bake thinly sliced fruit for snacks, saving some for pies in winter months.

Fried Peach Pies

Makes 12

CRUST

2 cups plus 2 tablespoons
    all-purpose flour
2½ teaspoons confectioners'
    sugar
¾ teaspoon kosher salt
¼ cup cold unsalted butter,
    cubed
¼ cup cold lard, cubed
½ cup ice water

FILLING

4 large fresh peaches,
    peeled, pitted, and
    finely chopped
½ cup firmly packed light
    brown sugar
2 tablespoons butter, melted
1 teaspoon vanilla extract
⅛ teaspoon kosher salt
⅛ teaspoon ground
    cinnamon
⅛ teaspoon ground nutmeg

Vegetable oil, for frying
Garnish: confectioners'
    sugar

CRUST In a large bowl, sift together flour, confectioners' sugar, and salt. Using a pastry blender, cut in butter and lard until mixture is crumbly. Sprinkle with ice water, 1 tablespoon at a time, tossing with a fork until a dough forms. Divide dough in half; shape into 2 disks. Wrap each in plastic wrap, and refrigerate for at least 2 hours.

FILLING In a medium saucepan, cook peaches, brown sugar, melted butter, vanilla, salt, cinnamon, and nutmeg over medium heat, stirring occasionally, until peaches are tender, about 30 minutes. Remove from heat; let cool completely.

On a lightly floured surface, roll half of dough to ⅛-inch thickness. Using a 4½-inch round cutter, cut 6 rounds. Repeat with remaining dough, rerolling scraps only once. Spoon 1 tablespoon peach filling onto center of each round. Fold dough over filling, and crimp edges with a fork to seal. Refrigerate for 1 hour.

In a large Dutch oven, pour oil to two-thirds full. Heat over medium heat until a deep-fry thermometer registers 350°. Fry pies, 3 at a time, until golden brown, 6 to 8 minutes, turning occasionally. Let drain on paper towels. Garnish with confectioners' sugar, if desired.

German Chocolate-Pecan Hand Pies

In a medium saucepan, bring pecans, sugar, corn syrup, melted butter, and eggs to a boil over medium heat. Reduce heat, and simmer for 10 minutes, stirring frequently. Remove from heat. Add chocolate, coconut, and vanilla, stirring until chocolate melts.

On a lightly floured surface, roll each piecrust to 1/8-inch thickness. Using a 4 1/2-inch round cutter, cut dough, rerolling scraps as necessary.

Preheat oven to 400°. Spray 2 baking sheets with cooking spray.

Transfer dough rounds to a clean flat surface. Brush edges of dough with egg yolk. Place a heaping tablespoon of chocolate mixture onto center of each round. Fold dough over filling, and crimp edges with a fork to seal. Place pies on prepared pans.

Bake until lightly browned, 15 to 18 minutes.

MAKES ABOUT 24

1½ cups chopped pecans
1 cup sugar
¾ cup light corn syrup
6 tablespoons butter,
  melted
3 large eggs
1 (4-ounce) bar
  German's sweet
  chocolate, chopped
1 cup sweetened flaked
  coconut
1 teaspoon vanilla extract
2 (14.1-ounce) packages
  refrigerated piecrusts
1 large egg yolk, beaten

Flaky and crispy on the outside and warm on the inside, hand pies are a sweet treat for afternoon tea time. For me, any season is better with these little gems.

Green Tomato Hand Pies

MAKES 12

**Basic Pie Dough
(recipe on page 10)**
½ cup finely chopped
toasted pecans
(optional)
½ teaspoon ground
nutmeg (optional)
2 medium green
heirloom tomatoes,
finely chopped
and drained
⅓ cup golden raisins,
finely chopped
¼ cup plus
3 tablespoons sugar,
divided
¼ teaspoon ground
cinnamon
¼ teaspoon kosher salt
⅛ teaspoon ground
nutmeg
1 large egg, lightly beaten
3 tablespoons heavy
whipping cream

Make Basic Pie Dough, adding pecans and nutmeg
to dry ingredients, if desired.

Preheat oven to 350°. Line a baking sheet with
parchment paper.

On a lightly floured surface, roll each dough disk
to ⅛-inch thickness. Cut 12 (4-inch) rounds and
12 (3½-inch) rounds. Place 3½-inch rounds on
prepared pan.

In a medium bowl, combine tomatoes, raisins, ¼ cup
sugar, cinnamon, salt, and nutmeg. Place a heaping
tablespoon of tomato mixture onto center of each
3½-inch round. Brush edges of each 4-inch round with
egg. Place 4-inch rounds over tomato mixture, and press
edges with a fork to seal. Brush dough with cream, and
sprinkle with remaining 3 tablespoons sugar.

Bake until golden brown, 20 to 25 minutes. Serve warm.

Frozen Peach-Blueberry Cobbler Bites

In a 12-cup muffin pan, spoon 2 tablespoons sorbet into each muffin cup. Using a spoon, spread in an even layer. Freeze until firm, about 20 minutes.

In a medium bowl, stir together ice cream, peach, and blueberries. Divide mixture among muffin cups, smoothing top with a spoon. Freeze until slightly firm, about 15 minutes.

Spread 2 teaspoons jam over ice cream in each muffin cup. Top each with 1 biscuit half. Cover muffin pan tightly with plastic wrap. Freeze overnight or for up to 3 weeks.

To remove from pan, dip bottom of pan in warm water for about 10 seconds. Run an offset spatula around edges of cups to loosen; invert onto a baking sheet. Garnish with whipped cream and blueberries, if desired.

MAKES 12

1½ cups peach sorbet, softened
1¾ cups vanilla ice cream, softened
1 fresh peach, peeled, pitted, and chopped
½ cup fresh blueberries
½ cup blueberry jam
6 prepared buttermilk biscuits, halved
Garnish: sweetened whipped cream, fresh blueberries

I have observed that there are three types of dessert people—chocolate, fruit, and custard or pudding types. I think I love all three! Who can say no to dessert? It's the great hoorah at the end of a meal!

Mini Strawberry Rhubarb Pies

MAKES 8

Basic Pie Dough
  (recipe on page 10)
3/4 **cup toasted shredded**
  coconut (optional)
1½ **tablespoons dried**
  lavender (optional)
4 **cups quartered fresh**
  strawberries
1¼ **cups chopped fresh**
  rhubarb
1 **cup sugar, divided**
4 **tablespoons tapioca flour**
½ **teaspoon salt**
Garnish: Coconut Whipped
  Cream (recipe follows),
  toasted coconut

COCONUT WHIPPED CREAM
MAKES ABOUT 2 CUPS

1 **cup heavy whipping cream**
3/4 **cup toasted shredded**
  coconut
¼ **cup confectioners' sugar**
¼ **teaspoon kosher salt**

Make Basic Pie Dough, adding coconut and lavender as dry ingredients, if desired. Preheat oven to 350°.

On a lightly floured surface, roll half of dough to ⅛-inch thickness. Using a 6-inch round cutter, cut 4 rounds. Transfer to 4 (4-inch) mini pie plates or soufflé dishes, letting excess dough extend over edges. Trim edges to ¼-inch beyond edge of plates. Fold edges under, and crimp as desired. Cover with plastic wrap, and refrigerate for 30 minutes. Repeat with remaining dough. Prick bottom and sides of dough with a fork. Place pie plates on a rimmed baking sheet.

Bake until edges are pale, 8 to 12 minutes.

In a large saucepan, cook strawberries, rhubarb, and ½ cup sugar over medium heat, stirring occasionally, until berries are tender, about 8 minutes. Strain fruit, reserving juice.

In a medium bowl, whisk together 1 cup reserved strawberry-rhubarb juice, tapioca flour, salt, and remaining ½ cup sugar. Add strawberry-rhubarb mixture to juice, stirring gently to combine. Pour into prepared crusts. Place pies on a rimmed baking sheet.

Bake until filling is bubbly and crust is golden, 20 to 30 minutes. Remove from pans, and let cool for at least 3 hours before serving. Garnish with Coconut Whipped Cream and toasted coconut, if desired

COCONUT WHIPPED CREAM

In a small saucepan, heat cream over medium heat until just beginning to bubble. Remove from heat, and add coconut. Let steep until cool, about 10 minutes. Strain cream, discarding coconut. Place in an airtight container, and refrigerate until very cold, about 2 hours.

In a medium bowl, beat coconut cream, confectioners' sugar, and salt with a mixer at medium speed until soft peaks form, about 3 minutes.

Mini Peach Cobblers

Preheat oven to 350°.

In a large saucepan, cook peaches, butter, orange juice, and lemon juice over medium heat, stirring occasionally, until butter is melted, about 8 minutes.

In a medium bowl, whisk together sugar, cornstarch, cinnamon, and nutmeg; stir into peach mixture until combined. Remove from heat.

Divide peach mixture among 6 (1½ cup) ovenproof dishes. Divide Almond Shortbread Topping over peach mixture. Place on a rimmed baking sheet.

Bake until browned and bubbly, 25 to 28 minutes.

ALMOND SHORTBREAD TOPPING In a large bowl, stir together flour, sugar, baking powder, and salt. Using a pastry blender, cut in butter until mixture is crumbly. Stir in almonds and cream just until combined. (Mixture will be crumbly.) Turn out dough, and shape into a disk. Wrap in plastic wrap, and refrigerate until ready to use.

MAKES 6

6 cups peeled, pitted, and sliced fresh peaches
2 tablespoons butter
2 tablespoons fresh orange juice
1 tablespoon fresh lemon juice
1 cup sugar
2 teaspoons cornstarch
½ teaspoon ground cinnamon
¼ teaspoon ground nutmeg
Almond Shortbread Topping (recipe follows)

ALMOND SHORTBREAD TOPPING
MAKES DOUGH FOR 6 MINI COBBLERS

½ cup plus 2 tablespoons all-purpose flour
¼ cup sugar
¾ teaspoon baking powder
½ teaspoon kosher salt
3 tablespoons cold unsalted butter, cubed
¼ cup sliced almonds
¼ cup heavy whipping cream

Mini Cherry Custard Pies

MAKES 4

1 (21-ounce) can cherry
   pie filling
1 large egg
¼ cup honey
1 lemon, zested and
   juiced
1 teaspoon vanilla
   extract
½ teaspoon ground
   cardamom
½ teaspoon ground
   cinnamon
1 (14.1-ounce) package
   refrigerated piecrusts
Garnish: whipped cream,
   fresh blueberries

Preheat oven to 350°. Spray 4 (6-ounce) mini pie pans or ovenproof dishes with cooking spray.

In a medium bowl, stir together pie filling, egg, honey, lemon zest, lemon juice, vanilla, cardamom, and cinnamon.

On a lightly floured surface, roll half of dough to ⅛-inch thickness. Using a 5-inch round cutter, cut 6 rounds. Roll remaining dough to ⅛-inch thickness, and cut 2 more rounds.

Place 1 round in each prepared pan. Divide filling among piecrusts. Using a small star-shaped cutter or a knife, cut a star in center of each remaining round. Place dough over filling, pressing edges to seal. Place on a baking sheet.

Bake until crust is lightly browned and filling is hot and bubbly, about 25 minutes. Let cool slightly before serving. Garnish with whipped cream and blueberries, if desired.

There are more than 300 unique types of honey produced from a different floral source. Orange Blossom nectar is lighter in color, where honey from wildflowers tends to be a dark golden color. Preserving flowering plants for the honeybee is good for all of us.

Fried Pecan Pies

CRUST In the work bowl of a food processor, pulse together flour and salt. Add butter and shortening; pulse until mixture is crumbly. Transfer mixture to a large bowl. Sprinkle with ice water, 1 tablespoon at a time, tossing with a fork just until dry ingredients are moistened.

Turn out dough onto a lightly floured surface, and gently knead until combined, 2 to 3 times. Shape into a disk, and wrap in plastic wrap. Refrigerate for 30 minutes.

FILLING In a medium saucepan, bring brown sugar, corn syrup, 3 tablespoons water, butter, and salt to a boil over medium-high heat. Reduce heat to low; simmer for 2 minutes. Remove from heat; stir in pecans and vanilla. Let cool for 20 minutes.

On a lightly floured surface, roll dough to ⅛-inch thickness. Using a 3½-inch round cutter, cut dough into 12 rounds. Brush edges of dough with water. Spoon 2 teaspoons pecan mixture onto center of each round. Fold dough over filling, and crimp edges with a fork to seal.

Fill a large skillet halfway full with oil. Heat over medium heat until a deep-fry thermometer registers 350°. Fry pies, in batches, turning occasionally, until golden brown, 3 to 5 minutes. Let drain on paper towels. Let cool for 10 minutes. Garnish with granulated sugar and cocoa, if desired.

MAKES 12

CRUST
2 cups all-purpose flour
1 teaspoon salt
¼ cup cold unsalted butter
¼ cup all-vegetable shortening
5 to 7 tablespoons ice water

FILLING
⅓ cup firmly packed dark brown sugar
⅓ cup dark corn syrup
3 tablespoons water
1 tablespoon butter
¼ teaspoon salt
1 cup chopped pecans
1 teaspoon vanilla extract

Vegetable oil, for frying
Garnish: granulated sugar, unsweetened cocoa powder

Raspberry Fried Pies with Chilled Vanilla Rum Sauce

MAKES 8

2 cups fresh raspberries
1/4 cup granulated sugar
2 tablespoons
cornstarch
1 tablespoon fresh
lemon juice
1 (16.3-ounce) can
refrigerated large
homestyle biscuits*
1 large egg, lightly beaten
Vegetable oil, for frying
Chilled Vanilla Rum
Sauce (recipe
follows)
Garnish: confectioners'
sugar

*We used Grands! Homestyle
Biscuits.*

CHILLED VANILLA
RUM SAUCE
MAKES ABOUT 2 CUPS

2 cups vanilla bean ice
cream, softened
1 tablespoon rum

In a small saucepan, stir together raspberries, granulated sugar, cornstarch, and lemon juice. Cook over medium heat, stirring constantly, until berries begin to release their juices and sugar and cornstarch dissolve. Remove from heat, and let cool completely.

On a lightly floured surface, roll each biscuit to 1/8-inch thickness. Spoon raspberry filling onto center of each biscuit. Brush edges of each biscuit with egg. Fold dough over filling, and crimp edges with a fork to seal.

In a medium saucepan, pour oil to a depth of 1 inch. Heat over medium heat until a deep-fry thermometer registers 350°. Fry pies, in batches if necessary, until golden brown, about 3 minutes per side. Serve with Chilled Vanilla Rum Sauce. Garnish with confectioners' sugar, if desired.

CHILLED VANILLA RUM SAUCE In a small bowl, stir together ice cream and rum. Cover and refrigerate for up to 3 days.

Recipe TIP

Use the tines of a fork or
a crimping tool to gently
press into the edges of the
dough, creating an even,
rippled trim.

Mini Strawberry Cobblers

Preheat oven to 350°.

In a medium bowl, toss together strawberries, ½ cup granulated sugar, 3 tablespoons flour, lemon juice, and cinnamon. Spoon strawberry mixture into 8 (6-ounce) ovenproof dishes.

In the work bowl of a food processor, pulse together brown sugar, butter, almond extract, remaining ¼ cup granulated sugar, and remaining ½ cup flour until crumbly. Fold in almonds. Sprinkle about ⅓ cup topping over each dish.

Bake until topping is golden brown and filling is thick and bubbly, about 30 minutes. Let cool slightly before serving.

MAKES 8

1 (32-ounce) container fresh strawberries, quartered
¾ cup granulated sugar, divided
½ cup plus 3 tablespoons all-purpose flour, divided
1 tablespoon fresh lemon juice
1 teaspoon ground cinnamon
¼ cup firmly packed light brown sugar
¼ cup cold butter
¼ teaspoon almond extract
¼ cup sliced almonds

Mini skillets make perfect individual pies. I like to top them with extra crumble ingredients and add a small scoop of ice cream with a sprinkle of cinnamon on top. A trend in serving, mini cast-iron skillets make a casual dining experience feel unique.

.recipe index.